A RAINBOW
THING WITH
WINGS

Seema Tangri

A Rainbow Thing With Wings

Copyright @ 2020

Seema Tangri

ISBN: 978—1–64953–045–5

Absolute Author Publishing House
New Orleans, LA

PRINTED IN THE UNITED STATES AMERICA

Absolute Author
Publishing House

Dedicated to

My loving and beautiful family:
Mariya Gencheva
Keranka Shopova
ArunKumar Narayanan
Madhav Arun
Naveen Tangri
Urmil Tangri
Jang Bahadur Tangri
And

My loving Lord, who has given me everything
Radha-Krishna
And

TO YOU,

LOVELY HUMAN:

YOUR EMOTIONS ARE GOLDEN, YOUR INTELLIGENCE IS

MAGIC, AND YOUR POTENTIAL IS UNLIMITED

Contents

The reason i'm writing this book is because I need the world to know something.

Everywhere I look, people are suffering from temporary sense enjoyment, from illness, from disturbances and diseases.

I need everyone around me to know the truth.

The force that creates the universe around us is pure, unconditional and undivided love. It is based in Bhakti, which is an unalloyed devotion.

It is my hope that this book plants a seed of awakening in you, dear reader. It is my hope that it waters the beauty that is already and forever present within your energy. You have never been created and will never be destroyed.

(The body is dust. From dust to dust, right? This is the nature of all things that are material. How can we glorify the material body, then? How can we identify with it?

＊

This is the single biggest mistake and misconception that we have allowed ourselves to entangle with over the years. This great misconception is the illusion of separation.)

So with that, dear reader, I send you off, into the magical lands of mental depths.

Enjoy, with love.

A BIRTHING
THING WITH
WINGS

To Begin-

I need everyone to wake up.

I refuse to see suffering here.

It is madness, it is a delusion.

-It is an Illusion

Truth is waiting for you.

There is no separation.

This is the only truth.

That is why love is the strongest—because it is all that exists.

When we try to concoct the illusion of separation – which results in envy as its first quality – we dig our own grave and then lie in it.

This is the greatest misuse of human life.

The false will always be false and the truth will always be true. This is the nature of the polarity between falsity and truth. Black and white.

Look at how fragile the body is. How can it be significant? It is dust. Temporary. Unreal.

Look at how fragile any material quality is.

This is exactly why we should resist the development of any sort of attachment to that which is nonpermanent, and develop an attachment to permanency instead.
This is the key.

So long as there is attachment, there is suffering. This is natural. Attachment implies something that is stuck, that thing that has an inability to move.
It is the antecedent of freedom.
Pure love requires freedom.

   -Back to Our Origin

To Continue:

Beings suffer so much in the material plane.

This is the nature of reaction: karma.

It must be done.

That's why you are here.

The universe operates perfectly. You need to be here, so you are here.

For now, living here must be done.

But, if you are blessed enough to take a human life, you have the highest form of material intelligence.

Meaning, you have the answer out of here. Embedded in your DNA.

My heart bursts with desperation.

It aches with surrender and the determination to free as many souls as God wills me to.

Compassion is needed to see every living being with equal

– 20/20

Anything that is not love is falsity.

That may be a long list of things.

It is time to be diligent.

On where our minds, hearts, and actions lie.

On our priorities.

On understanding that we are directly tied to love personified.

– *Abandoning Illusion*

Furthermore,

I need you to listen to the voice that flows through you when you're alone.

Silent.

Not thinking.

Just listening.

That voice is pure magic.

How does the brain have the capacity to form an internal voice? To speak and listen at the same time?

It is the most remarkable thing.

-Duality

But for now,

Don't think about that.

Don't think about anything.

Just listen. Observe.

–Naturally

✷

The universe is constantly trying to communicate with us
-- in messages, in music, in people.
And it operates on the language of love.

I need all of you to know about the power that is love.
I need you to know that I - as a separate personality from
you - do not exist.
Your name is the label, your body is the vehicle, and your
consciousness is the connection.

You are the expression of the whole universe embodied in a
single fragmental part.
Like the entire ocean in a drop of water.
Except the ocean doesn't have an end to its' outward
expansion.
And the drop doesn't have an end to its' inward.

I need you to know that you and I are the same.

Abandon your identification with your perceived self.
You are all that is Unperceived.
You are perfect because you can never be created nor
destroyed.
You are acting in this expression for the service - and of the
will - of the Creator.

   –Discernment

When we lose ourselves in focus, that is when we harness our highest potential of energetic power.

Focus is our greatest asset.

The ability to harness all of our mental and emotional willpower to create is the definition of manifestation.

We have the Creator in us, and so, it is our inclination to create. All things.

We create emotion, we create fantasy, we create physicality, and we create other beings.

This is the nature of transmutation itself.

We harness this power throughout daily life already.

But now we must become conscious of it - and use it to create what we want in our lives.

What is the goal of human life?

Ideally, it is experience (to learn), and then transcendence - to apply what has been learned.

 —Two Step Process

It is important that one pay attention to how their movements are.

If one is swift and steadfast, then they must work to be calm and cool, so that there is balance.

If one is slow and deliberate, then they must attempt at being more quick.

This is the nature of perfect balance.

—Neither Here Nor There

The many beings of material life are suffering very strongly with the six senses, which include the mind.

When humans do nothing but indulge in sense gratification and consume according to that standard, there is a great danger.

Weariness and age come faster, and the mind becomes slow. Fulfilling the six senses, which include the mind, becomes the primary focus.

And all self-control is lost.

− Truth is Our Power

＊

Self-control breeds proper focus.

Without the necessary self-control to be able to distinguish what should be done on this material plane and what should not be done,

     one

          becomes

               lost.

The lost individual risks entangling themselves into illusion, which is all around us, and from which envy arises.

The birth of envy is the death of love.

For it is from here that we begin to think we are separate beings.

Proper focus in life means being very serious about self-realization.

It requires silence, introspection, to separate oneself from the general population, to allow for growth and change, to abandon certain lifestyles and habits to make room for new ones, and to live with a primary driving force, or purpose.

– One Point Gaze

We find our purpose when we find ourselves.

Our purpose will always be for a positive reason.

Our purpose will always be in line with our core beliefs and values.

Our purpose will always inspire us to grow and change.

Our purpose will always be an uncomfortable, but necessary, adjustment.

Our purpose will always help others in some way.

Our Creator gives us our purpose.

Our Creator will always be the highest amount of happiness/bliss we will ever receive or experience.

Our Creator is never temporary, is everywhere, is the knower of all things, is fractal, and is simultaneously always a person.

—You Are Both My Mother and Father

The personable qualities of our Creator is what enables us to cultivate a loving affection for all beings.

One with an equal eye sees all living beings as qualitatively the same, possessing the same energy substance.

Therefore, with equal vision, this individual speaks sweetly and truthfully, treads lightly, eats cleanly, does not make judgments about others, performs their duty, and in doing so, does not incur heavy karmic reactions.

—Sweet Person-ability

The speed at which we move forward is the speed with which we shall progress.

It is up to us.

Our free will is very limited, as we cannot control the position of the sun and whether it rises or sets.

But what we can control, we must.

The place most suitable and necessary for control is the internal space below where our consciousness dwells.

The conscious mind is at the forefront of the subconscious, and therefore requires constant grooming, updating, and attention.

–Software Boost

✳

What we focus on grows.

This is the nature of how energy itself works.

Energy goes where attention flows.

The way to live a meaningful, purposeful, and authentic life is to pay attention to stay focused on acting through loving devotional service, giving everything we do, think, say, are, and breathe, unto Source.

–Be Careful

To heal, we must be in a state of healing.

Time is the destroyer of all things.

It exists as a governor over the temporary.

The past is a figment, and the future is un promised.

The only thing that really exists is the present moment.

Therefore, to create our future, we must do it now.

– Our Power

✴

And if you are ever sad, confused, or mislead on who exactly
it is you are living your life for,
I want you to go to a mirror,
Stand there,
And look very deep inside of that being that you see.
The powerhouse of energy that pours through every
pulsating of your heart --
 That's who.

 – Electric Currents

✺

I think the coolest thing about us is that
You can eradicate any thought that you want to if you don't
like it.
If you don't like it, the second that you want it gone, it can
be gone.
Your head is your house.

Once you realize the power you harbor
When you become very clear on what thoughts you give
even a split moment's attention towards --
Then you do, by default, become very clear.
Crystal clear.
You structure your life around this clarity,
And this is called stability.

– Attention

Motivation is up to you, and the best for you.

It is yours to be bold with.

This is your life to build.

When you take control of your inner world, you water only those plants you want in your garden.

Weeds will go,

Roses will grow,

And you will understand

That this life is a never-ending pool of excitement.

Of new people, new places, new fantasies, new endeavors, new goals, new emotions --

And overall,

So so much

To learn.

This is the beauty of life.

—Choose Your Own Adventure

Life is morning protein shakes and "to do" lists.

Life is learning to astral-project and exploring the limits of your subconscious.

Life is forcing yourself to fall in love with better habits.

Life is being above your mind,

So now,

YOU write

The rules.

—*Autonomy*

Do it for your own mental strength.

Delve through every corner of your personality until you understand

Who you are ?

What you need ?

And where you're going ?

Everyone can do it

Not everyone chooses to

But those who do

Gain from the darkness, the brightest light

Of humility

Of gratitude

Of peace imbedded in bliss.

– Lighthouse

None of your money is yours
Neither is your body
And neither are your worries
Each day we are born again
If we choose to be.

—Reincarnation

In the material world, it helps to be coachable.

There are powerful influences all around you,

Ready and willing to help you be the best version of yourself.

It is up to you

To see the bright lantern of opportunity

Everywhere you look.

—You Get What You Look For

You have been with Source before.

It doesn't matter when.

We all have.

We all are.

Constantly.

For Source is time personified.

−Millenia

Health is wealth.

Here's why:

Money can be recovered. Yes, even health can be recovered.

Time can be remembered.

But a particular state of health under the exact influence of a particular time -

Now that can never be brought back.

—Fated Incident

Thinking, planning, and doing are three very different actions of execution.

Like three legs of a stool

All necessary,

And each one at a particular time.

It serves the magician well to know which tool on the table to use,

And when.

–Holy Trinity

✴

Do everything with a purpose.

From your thoughts to your speech, to your actions.

The purpose behind action,

Sets the intention for the action.

Intention is energy,

And energy never lies.

—So Decide

Chances are, you are your own guru.

We all need a spiritual coach to take reference from

But the same love that is within everyone,

Is within you too;

All you have to do

Is See It.

  –Third Eye

Service is the highest form of action.

There is no possible way it can generate any negative karma.

Therefore, if there is anything you must learn how to do here,

It is how to lovingly serve -

With devotion,

And intention.

–For You

Use what you have to get what you want.

This is the nature of alchemy.

Use your strength, your spirituality, your flexibility

Use everything you have —

They are gifts.

Break the mold and keep your head above the water.

You can float if you lie on your back.

—Buoyancy

When you have a mission, you don't ever stop. You can't. The sky is the limit. There is no limit. When you have a mission to God, you will go as far as you keep remembrance, humility, and urgency. The rest of your life will always start now. As long as you are here, you move.

—*Limitless*

When you don't feel like moving forward,

or are resisting something new from happening,

this is the time where you most crucially need to hold on to

your strength,

and even more importantly - to triumphantly keep walking.

Go.

You're good.

—Get Up

New chapters are beautiful new beginnings

It is important not to have any expectations whatsoever–
        good or bad.

Live in the moment, where you are not expecting and not
waiting.

You simply

Are.

What a beautiful thing it is–when you do

what you came here to do:

Experience.

–Flow

God will not give you anything

That you cannot

Eventually

Handle.

(It's through handling that we are becoming).

  —Strength-building

It's only through losing your focus that you can become fearful.

Otherwise, it's not possible.

You've already faced all the lessons that you've needed to learn.

You already have tasted the sweet nectar of inventive creation
And inventive building.

Your palms have been itching to -not only create- but to display

So now, please, child,

Elate in your production play.

     —Stagetime

Everything you do is golden

Faith gives you strength

Strength is not a phenomenon that is a byproduct of fear

Strength is a product on its own

Originally

Needing no prerequisites or allowances

You do not need to have strength in hard times

You need to have strength all the time

For the smart are strong

And they practice it religiously

   —*Without Conditions*

The smart are strong because they learn

That they have to be

That they have learned to be

That they originally are

That strength is the truth

And fear

Is

The

Illusion

    —Survival

Human emotions are guidebooks

Why would you not read your own guidebook

Exploring its pages

With depth and tenderness

And a type of devotion that comes from not this Earth

And in the dedication, on the front

It says "For Our Creator"

The one that is consistently

Maintaining

And

Destroying

Over and over again.

—Maps

I am not political

My only politics is the one thing that resides above the highest of all intelligence

The forever-spoken language

Of unconditionality and eternity:

Love

—Main Mantra

I do not engage in thoughts that are lesser than what I
deserve

This is self-protection

This is sweet focused loving awareness

On what is wanted for you

And it is important to remember, too,

That whatever we're given

Is also

Wanted

For us

—Ordained

The only One who has the complete capacity to know your
heart entirely
Is always
Conveniently
Listening.

    —No Need To Hide

I am a girl, but only in one aspect of myself
I am tall, but only from one perspective
I am sweet, but only because I have inherited this genetically
I am stubborn for the same reason.

I love very deeply, and so I do my duty.
But not all the time, and not always well.
I am filled with a consciousness
That is a never-ending paradox
And a spiral

And a tunnel
Of all sorts of odd galaxies
And so are
You

–Paradoxical

✷

Faith is very important

Without faith, we don't know priority.

And without priorities, we don't know intention.

Without intention, we don't know our direction.

And

Direction determines everything.

—Have Faith

My life isn't a popularity contest

I don't care about that.

I care about the opposite of that, which is my inward strength and stability.

I care about the karma I need to fulfill.

I care about my work, my loving service, and how much I value I can give while I'm here.

I am on a mission, and missions require steadfastness.

There is no time

To waste.

—Opposite Of That

✴

Be patient.

For what was written for you

Was written by the Greatest of Writers.

—Destiny

✱

The law of happiness is that it has nothing to do with external circumstances,
only internal conditions.

–Regulation

✳

The first rule of making new memories:
Don't dwell on old ones.

   —Move On

You take control of yourself and your life

By taking control of your mind

Have purpose with every step.

Every

Moment

Counts

And it's beautiful.

You've been through worse.

No matter what,

You've been through worse.

You're prepared.

The best is yet to come.

−Chin Up

A businessman counts his losses

And moves forward

Because he knows the value

Of forward movement.

—I Will Never Be Stagnant

I love a good strategy

I love a good dose of discipline

It's the spark before the fire

The seed before the tree

And the pregnancy period

For a lot of solid invention

−Conception

✳

I love a good lovely love

A sweet one, without strongholds

Labels or no labels

Our love is boundless

By time or space

A brush stroke here, a glitter drop there

I love the way our colors blend

Your originality and my uniqueness

You pour and I pour

Together

We have no shortage

Of Abundance to give

You sing and I watch you with stars in my eyes

Listening carefully and laughing with ecstasy

A good lovely love

Gives me enough hope for the whole world

There is no gap between us,

This is the stuff of the Gods.

—Abstract Art

One more time I want to write about you

Just one more time, for now

My logical brain tells me i'm placing you on a pedestal

I don't care - I built it myself.

The idea of you is no different from you,

And I know this because the idea of you sparkles.

Look how free you allow your voice to wander

I'm struck with admiration, and it doesn't leave me for the
rest of the day.

Watching your soul fly feels like i'm flying

I normally wouldn't allow myself feel this way

I don't think I will tomorrow.

But for now, until the music ends

I'll join you on your pedestal

Into the sky

—Indulgence

I stopped caring what people think

Because that meant

Ignoring what I think

And i'm the one who lives in my brain

Not you

And i'm the one who is responsible for my body

And how well taken care of it is

And i'm the one responsible

For the entire life

I have yet to live

—Power

Knowledge is power

On its own,

Useless.

But turning knowledge into wisdom

Is applying that power

And using it

For your Life

Moment

after

moment.

–Taking Action

Healthy boundaries
That's the key to clean living
With this in mind
I can be as dynamic as I am
I can be fierce
And soft
All at the same time
One body
Many minds

—*MultiFaceted*

It doesn't matter how I look

That's not who I am

I could look soft

With a tsunami over the sand

I could look fierce

With a heart like a deer's

And a voice that sings a lot

And healing hands

How I look is often forgotten

I gaze in the mirror and jump back

So there's a face to that world

And she has eyes, a nose, and lips

That do the whispering of other lands.

–Who I Am

I used to live in fear
of being myself
because I was afraid
No one would like me.
I was afraid
Always afraid
I wanted to be
What people wanted from me

Now I am an empty vessel
For His molding
I use my ego
My ego doesn't use me
And I use it for the purpose
That I came here to receive
I don't care if people like me
I care if they like themselves
Because we all need healing
And we all can grow upward
Infinitely

—How I Pour

My intensity

Is the thing I love most about me

It seeps in through the spaces between my thoughts

Softening and guiding me

It forces my heart to open

And protects me against stagnancy.

It keeps a quiet fire lit

With a pale peach glow

Always ready to create

Always wanting to commit.

It creates a channel for me

to sit in silence and rejoice

for in between the collected thoughts

Are steadily flickering bits.

–But Don't Tell Anyone

✶

I don't think I'm a romantic.

At least, I hope not.

Romantics do this thing where they fantasize a lot.

And I certainly don't think

About the radiance in your smile

Or how your fingers create art

When they strum on your guitar

No, I don't think about that

I don't even think about the part

where you see the world so sweetly

And with so much heart

No, I would never.

That wouldn't be right

For my heart to capture you

it's like a bird without its flight

And what kind of bird doesn't fly?

That must be a really timid bird.

One that's pretty shy.

—Vibrations

Inspiration is probably the sweetest nectar my soul has ever
tasted

There is nothing that can compare to the imagination that
lies in creation

I want to eat it with my fingers and let it drip down my chin

I make a mess everywhere, this is part of the fun

I'm in my own world where no one can get in

Come with me! Do you see what I see?

A long list of dreams that reaches the sun

—Honey and Gold

＊

You've visited my brain again and made yourself comfortable there

I don't know why you don't just say something

I won't wait, but I won't house you either

I would gladly welcome you if you would just announce yourself first

There's a room for you upstairs and the bed is made

I won't disturb you, i'm very respectful

But I may ask you a few times if you want to lay out on the porch with me

We can watch the stars and talk about some dreams

Not all of them though; I don't give myself away

But if you want to, that's wonderfully okay

I'll entertain you and make you laugh

And you'll let me talk a lot

Time doesn't exist anyway

–On A House In The Sky

It is most imperative and most wise to be in a state of
ecstatic peace
It is only through this state that we can lovingly serve with
devotion
So either we attain towards service first
Or towards other means of raising our vibration to attain
that peace
Either one is fine
Because once we have one
We automatically have the other
And they feed each other
In constant circulation

−A Human's Potential

Religion is meant

For attaining the mode of goodness

Because from the mode of goodness

We can transcend the modes of material nature

(Goodness, passion, and ignorance)

All of the modes are entangled together

Like the sky is unseparated from the breeze

    —Entanglement

To my dear friend:

You're the second person i've written poetry about so forgive me if it's not pristine.

I forgot the way your eyes glisten when you speak and how they intensify right before you finish a sentence
And how they dart back and forth against mine insistently
I've missed that so much about you
They're like two big green marbles in a sea of peach tones
Moving with the smoothness of a
Suave
White
Cat
I've missed your infectious laugh and the way you make up words
You think it's weird and I live for it
I make you laugh and that makes me gleam with pride
Actually, you laugh at everything and so do I
I'm so glad I met you
Your heart is gentle and stubborn and strong and it's obvious
I see myself in you and you give me strength.

–Green Marbles

It's not about what you've been through

Or where you've been

As much as it is

Where you're going

    —The Road to All Success

The relationship one has with God is of spiritual nature,
and is the most relevant one we can ever engage in,

Because it is eternal.

Similarly, we should spend our lives focusing on developing
spiritual relationships - with Self, with others, and with our
work - all by keeping The Eternal in mind.

Only then will our lives be of relevance.

Only then will we live our Truth.

—Eternality

＊

Just as you have all forms,
When I remember You I feel Your potency -
And it transcends the realm
Of all
Space
And
Time

—*Potency*

✳

Do not make the mistake of labeling yourself ever.

You will come to realize that no label can ever come to pay your price.

The very definition of infinity is that which has no bounds.

—Definition of Infinity

✳

A CHIRPING THING WITH WINGS

Keep God close and work.

Then, you will carry love with you in all that you do.

As a result, nothing you do will ever be of ill nature

Or intent.

-Carry Love

✴

I think of you and all my worries fall away.

You are the relinquisher of all things painful, negative, or unholy.

—*Relinquisher*

Become comfortable with your mind

By cleaning the space often–it is your home after all, and

The thoughts that live there

Must be

Invited

Guests,

Only.

     –Invited Guests

You needn't ever have fear.

But if you do, that's okay.

Admit it, face it, so you can learn it -

And know that it's unnecessary.

Fear is opposite from love,

So if love is Truth,

Fear

Is

Illusion

—Fear

I am missing loving you closely.

My Lord, I am Yours, but you will never be mine.

All I want is simply to have the fortune to adore You.

Blessed am I, fortunate and exalted am I, to be able to remember You.

You are incomparable. Your splendor is not suited to be described in this world.

It is through loving you that I am set free from this material bondage.

−Exalted

God always helps those who need Him, because knowing that we need Him is surrendering onto Him - like a child asking for its mother in need.

The love we receive when we ask, without any ego, for help - this love is so strong that we carry it with us in our soul's memory for all eternity.

—Surrender

You swim somewhere in the large abyss of my thoughts

Waiting for me to find you,

You rest there.

Always helpful. Always merciful. Always there.

The second I forget my eternal connection with You is the second I fall.

If you are not the reason for my every breath, breathing loses meaning.

–Ocean of Mercy

✴

If you're going to put all your hopes and dreams somewhere, don't put them into a person.
Don't even put them in yourself.
Put them in the future of the life of the whole collective of humanity.

—Wise Investments

People are like different planets

That revolve

Around

Giving and receiving

Pull and push

Much like the

Tides

Of all the cosmic oceans

—Positive One and Negative One Equate to a Steady Zero

The thing that is black and blue

That looks like a bruise

Reminds me of You

With this note, I pay my final respects

To all the things inside me that have taught me

When a lesson is learned,

The teacher disappears.

So no more will I need any reminder of anything that I am not.

I refuse to be a victim of life's circumstances.

It was not abuse,

It was a blessing in disguise,

And it brought me to you.

—Black and Blue

No one deserves pain,

But this is karma.

The universe has to balance itself perfectly

As many times over as necessary.

Make no mistake.

If you suffered, it was not to hurt you, but to teach you.

The best lessons are taught with the most discipline.

And always from the best Teacher.

—School is in Session

If You are the largest of the large,

And the smallest of the small,

Then you are the fierceness that runs through my veins

When I decide to not give up at all.

I choose love so deeply that when I cry, all the three worlds

cry with me.

They know my resolve.

–Fractality

It's about knowing that He will deliver by His design, and
being at peace because of this knowledge.
And better yet,
We have been given everything -
So we ask
For nothing
At all

—Abundance

✴

I am the life-force behind the human physical body.

The body uses this life-force energy which is derived

From that which is Energetic.

Let me never forget this

Noble truth, of understanding

The make-up of my soul.

 —The Powerhouse of all Cells

Science

Is another word for

Creation

Is another word for

The

Source

The Beginning

Of All That Exists

And The End

Of All that Is No More

So,

There is no separation

Between Science

And Source.

−Unity

Do not worry for all that which is encouraging illusory activity.

That is the purest form of wisdom to remember,

And it has no prerequisites.

Attach yourself to the Eternal, and the illusory will fall away.

Discernment is yours.

–Own It

✳

The beauty of one who has love for the Universe is so transparent,

That it touches everyone in a way

That is pleasing

And nourishing

To the soul.

        Suddenly,

            Every action

                Is turned

                    Pure,

               Shiny,

          and

Exalted.

    —Radiance

Love does not have any

       judgements.

We cannot have purity in the same place we have

contamination.

So shed your skin, my love.

You have

      Layers

          and Layers

            and Layers

And beneath it all

            Is untouched light,

                Just waiting

          To Shine.

     —Dazzling

The greatest thing

A human being can do for themselves

Is to begin the journey

Of the Self.

Through Self-Discovery, we come Back,

Back,

Back,

To the

Original

Source

of all Creation.

—We Are Here For Our Souls To Grow

*

Sweet discipline,

How much I cherish your square edges.

You attempt to solidify that which is etheric,

You angle that which is soft and round.

The yang to my yin,

You are the action behind thought.

The fifth day of the week,

The road to harvest season.

You keep me in line, in check, in balance,

Stability has neither rhyme or reason.

The highest form of self-love,

My soulmate and forever partner,

For you are my God-given power.

Beautiful actions follow your intent,

For my soul is free,

But you help me cultivate it.

—*Discipline*

In the Bhagavad-Gita it says,

It is better to do your own duty improperly than another's duty properly.

So when I was eight,

And I fell off my bike and scarred my knee for life

I had no regrets.

And when I was eighteen,

And failed my first college course,

Instead of questioning myself and my ability,

I knew there would be a next time,

And I had no regrets.

For as long as we are alive,

There will always be another chance to get up, to

Dust
Off

And to try again.

For to perform our duty properly is a gift hand-picked for us.

—Eccentricity

101

The constellations

    Are not more outside of us

        Than they are coursing through our veins

    Each Nakshatra

Powering us

    In a way that is best suited

For the life-breath

    Of our soul.

    –Star Stuff

The thing about a spiritual journey

Is that you don't go anywhere

Rather, you cycle back within yourself

Over

And over

And over

Until you realize

That lessons that are not learned are repeated

And so actually we are all scholars

Studying very hard

And very enthusiastically

For the Final Exam.

In this school, however,

No one fails

We all get a second chance.

And we all realize our Selves.

—*Good Luck*

✴

Spirituality

    Is the

        Consistent

           Language

             Of

                The

                  Ancient

                     Soul

—Multilingual

It is not that we are born into a human body,
And we stay
And we lay
And we don't really question anything at all.

It is not that we are born into a human body,
And we accept the degradation of it.

We were not meant to work for the solidification of the land,
But rather,
The solidification of our hearts.

Soil is tilled for generations
And still yet,
Nothing is stirred in man.

Man has all the stirrings a tornado inside his heart
With all the depth of
All the galaxies
Milky Way itself becomes liquidated,
Riding through his bloodstream.

Man is short for hu-man,
The beings that self-realize
Because they are the only ones that can.

Even more dominion we should have over our egos,
Rather than the soil of the land.
For nature is the man's woman.

   —The Art of Living

Please, I beg you.

With folded hands and folded knees,

Embrace love like there is nothing else worth it here.

Embrace it like your life depends on it.

Because it does!
A life of love!
Is the only life worth living,
Uncontaminated by the coarseness of the material flesh,
Unbound by space or time.

You Are.
That's it, you just are.
And that's enough for you to open your heart.
Hearts don't need prerequisites,
They don't need rules.
They don't need conditions.
Hearts are the most fun to create,
And they are God's favorite form of art.

—Energy Is Never Created Nor Destroyed

How many things do we do to keep us bound in repetitive cycles, or thought patterns?
I'm not going to be easy with you, reader.
Not on this one.
Look deep.
Deeper.
What's in there?
Do you like it?
Do you want it to stay?

Think about it.
You can exist in any way you want to exist.
And you exist in your brain any way,
So do you want to exist in there?

Don't get upset, or annoyed.
I'm just asking you to question it.
I love you very much because you are just like me,
And you too can sit down on your green Lillypad (it's a beagbag chair, but still) and answer your questions about life.

I choose to do mine through manuscript.
But you have a unique way to do it.

What's in there?
Reminder:
It's beautiful. Even if it's a little messy.
We like messy.
Cleaning up is the fun part.

–Professional Maid

Your originality is what inspires me.
Just the way you're able to tune into yourself and then not worry.
You strum with precision and care.
You are nervous, I can tell, but that makes it even better.
The notes are inventive, every single one of them.
You have your own style.
You sing with passion, through till the end,
The way a runner runs a mile.

I'm reminding myself to sing along with you,
To match you, in a style that only I can.
And we do.
Harmonies echo throughout my room,
Suddenly we're both onstage.

Bam.

I'm melting into each note, and you are skillfully riding them.
Two surfers, each with their own little
Ebb and flow.
I catch your eye and we both laugh a little.
We're onstage!

The tide is perfect now,
With waves gentle but strong.
We carry the crowd with us,
Into the heart of our song.

They love it there, everyone's in bliss,
Recounting the Most High
With hearts, minds, and mouths open,
The world fiercely sings along.

    —Song of Our Hearts

We have been taught

Our whole lives

That it is unsafe to love.

When in reality, the only unsafe part about this life is fear.

Fear is opposite love, which means

That anything that is not love is fear.

And therefore, illusion.

This is the formula for living properly, authentically, happily, and with great joy, charisma, and innocence in our hearts.

We all have a child inside that has been traumatized by different fears.
A sweet child, whose personality has been split
Due to the various conditionings of this material world.

Truly, the natural way of life is the most appropriate,
But more than anything, we need to be natural in the soul.
There is no way to sugarcoat this.

First healing that glow and then radiating it,

And then discipline your life to follow it,

Always honoring and listening to it,

And never shutting your heart.

   —*It Is Safe To Love*

There is a lot of benefit that comes with disciplining the mind.
It's like cleaning your room.

And getting rid of the cobwebs in the corner, and putting
plants there instead.

Setting up a bright hot pink neon light in the center of the room,
For the vibes to be immaculate.

We don't like the curtains with graffiti all over them, or the
shattered mirror, so we replace both, fixing both our sense of
Sight and Self.

We know that no one else is going to do this job for us.
And that it imperative that we complete this task,
And update it whenever necessary.

We take pride,
When we restock the closet
With fresh, laundered goods.

We sing a song of freedom, as we air out the hallway,
Doors open to the unending realm of possibilities.

I am happy here.
When things are need and orderly.
When I know that life can turn upside down any day, in any
way.
And still,
I have my stability.

      —Mental Autonomy

✦

The beauty of a voice that is heard

Echoes across thousands of lifetimes.

We are not paper people

In paper towns

With paper dreams –

We are worlds within worlds,

Combined, making up an army,

Of spiritual beings, that are inside

Paper bodies

That crumble in the hands of time.

But we are not paper people,

Governed by any internal or external emotion.

Rather, we are universes!

Expanding and collapsing back within ourselves,

Back,

      Back,

            Back,

      Only for our light to be brought forward.

–Paper Dreams

We are not these bodies,

Nor are we the effects of the body.

Youth or agedness,

     Happy or sad,

         Right or left,

             Black or white.

The consistency is the same.

It's like going to a donut shop and finding out that

Inside each pastry

Is the same great explosion

Of sweet, tart, berries.

—Berries

＊

Human beings need love, not constant instruction.

Instruction cannot heal us, only love can.

Because it is love that the soul is so desperately yearning for.

And if we don't give and receive it, we start to become blind to it.

The love that is ever-present all around us,

Calling our names,

Calling our hearts,

I'm here,
I'm here,
I'm here,
Can't you see me?
                              Just open your eyes!
Everything else will fall into place.
          The heart must be open for our life to have meaning.
It doesn't have to take long,

          It can take

                    Two
                         Seconds:

                              One,
                                   Two,

               Bam.

          —Two Seconds

✦

A FALLING THING WITH WINGS

You can do anything you want to do

***

And be anything you want to be
The strongholds of the mind are not as strong
as all of the mysteries of the universe –
One of which is you.

—*Mysteries*

✴

No.

I will not allow you to confuse yourself with the human flesh you occupy.

One of these things is material,

While the other is eternal

So the next time

You lay stranded on the floor of your room

Wondering what in the galaxy to do,

Possibilities of demise and discouragement

Laid out in front of you

I want you to remember

That the galaxy you talk to

Is within you

Is without you

Is yourself you

And that all the stars in the universe

With admiration watch over you

Knowing you

To be one of their own.

–Kin

✳

It breaks my heart--
Have you ever seen a rose been plucked of all its petals?
That's how violently it breaks my heart--
Leaving it barren and wilted
When I am in suffering

My greatest cause of suffering
Is to look around
And see acres of potential rosebushes
Hanging like skeletons
Petals in the dirt

I have to do something to fix this,
So I begin picking up as many petals as I can
Only to realize
There is nothing in all the three worlds
As strong as nature's glue

Only the individual
Can regrow their petals again
Covering the once-barren bones
Of the foundation of their soul

And the only thing I can do
Is water
      Water
           Water.

    –Gardens

One step at a time
That's how we all learned to walk
That's certainly how I was taught,
Sun shimmering on the living room carpet
As my grandfather led me closer to the stairs

One step in front of the other
No focus on time
No focus on why
No focus on when
Or what maybe if then.

This is the meaning of zen.
One step,
Then another,
Then another.

No focus on past or future,
No focus on that which is figment.

There is only

Now.
And now.

                And now.

    –Slowly

＊

Yes,
I have been through a lot.
I have had thorns in my mind that I couldn't shake off.
I have had dust in my lungs
from the pollution in my heart.

But I went through a lot.
That's a very long tunnel,
With a very bright light at the end,
That for a long time
Was a very small dot.

I was there when the dot became the size of a
Grape
And then a
Grapefruit
A long and difficult pregnancy
Gave birth to a beautiful creation.

Now I am watching myself be cradled
By the limbs of the Milky Way
Encompassing me gently and tightly
Reminding me of the Divine play.

  —Rebirth

✻

You are past the personality you have
Oh so carefully crafted
With great painstaking attention
To the details that keep you tangled
In weeds as tall as the rays of the sun.

That is not what you are made of,
The crafting and the worries.
You are made of generational
Blood, sweat, and tears,
All sacrifices for your higher evolvement.

You are made of ancestral magic
Combined with personal freedom
And a whole lot of spirit –
All wrapped up in the emotion behind your eyes
That so beautifully captures
The articulations of your soul.

You are past the personality you have,
That can be changed
You are the surrender inside of the surrender
For the purity, the childishness,
It doesn't know pain.

–Pure

If I don't close my eyes
I will have no idea who I am.

The way I look in the mirror
Is different than the way I look on camera
Is different than the way I look in person
Is different than the way Eye Look.

If I don't close my eyes
I will get swept away
By winds of comparison
And talons of self-betrayal.

Why do I look like that?
I can scrutinize all day
And by nightfall
My nose would have shifted
And my face would have lifted
And I would have turned into play-dough.

    —Body Dysmorphia

✸

Jealousy
Is a two-headed viper snake
Each one wants to bite the other
Until there is nothing left.

  —*Avoiding Self-Demise*

Fantasy is all fun and games
Until an awakening so rude
It shakes you to the grave.

I remind myself that you are just a figment,
You are not in front of me so you are not real,
And I pretend to justify my play.

Why then,
Does my heart beat like that?
I told it to shut up
And it just beat even louder.
Is this how stubborn I am?
Even my brain has given up trying to reason with it --
It can't even catch up.

It tries yelling. Screaming.
But it's drowned out by the beating.
Like two rhythmic drums --
Rastafarian dreaming.

    —*Misleading*

I am not afraid of anything.
I have looked fear in the face and told it to go away,
Banishing it forever into foreign lands,
Never to return or stay.

I am not afraid of you.
I am not afraid of you.
I am not afraid of you.

You have access to my vulnerability,
And still, I am not afraid of you.
My vulnerability makes me strong.
There is nothing I don't open my heart to.

I had to mature very quickly.
Very quickly.
Name any mental anguish in the world.
I had it all.

So many times I could have slipped away
Quietly in the night,
Out of sight,
Under a guise of white hot bathroom lights.

I am not afraid of anything.
I am not afraid of loving you.
I am not even afraid of telling you.

But I am a girl
Who knows what she wants
And what she deserves.
So I have my eyes set on a prize,
And I am not afraid to respect my pride.

—Courage

The colors in front of my face
Shift in and out again
I remind myself that this is just a phase
This is just one of those moments,
The one with the daze.

I get up and immediately start doing jumping jacks,
Hoping that my eyes can refocus on something right in front
of my face.

Slowly, they do, and I can feel my feet becoming heavy again.
I made it back down.
I keep jumping, with my eyes fixed on a point ahead of me.
"Whatever it takes."

Maybe I just need water, I think,
And proceed to chug a jug.
At this point I'm flushed, with an ocean inside my place.

Maybe I just need to go outside.
So I do.
The trees whisper to me as I stand beneath them:
"Child, we feel it too."

I walk around the block, easing into the feeling of being
separate from
Space and time.
I roll with it, sometimes walking, sometimes skipping,
sometimes sitting on a bench and staring into nothing.
To you, I look crazy.
To me, I know I am.

    –Dissociation

Sometimes I feel like I'm a million years old.
I know for a fact I haven't done this earth thing before.
I'm from somewhere else
And I'm going back there after this
But while I'm here, I really hope I can live a life full of love.

There's no other way to live!
I'm convinced.
But then I think of romantic love,
And I freeze.

Why do I see it like that?
As something so scary, and dark, and cold.
Where I'm from, we don't have romantic love.
That's what the humans have sold.

Where I'm from – wrap your mind around this.
There's no such thing as possession or ownership.
But then I come here
And things are done so differently.
Life is about possession.
What kind of life is that?
That's no way to live!

But then I think of you,
And I freeze.
No answers come to me.
Now what do I do?
I do not want to possess you.
I want to love you.
But I'm already doing that.
So now what?

   —I Really Can't Wait To Go Home

I made the mistake
Of giving my heart to you
And not telling you about it
So now you're using it as a pick for your guitar
Creating beautiful music
At my expense

I'm just kidding
I'm so dramatic

I was also just kidding about being dramatic
I'm sure you have many more picks to use
From hearts given that you have yet to choose.

–*Strumming*

Nothing was enjoyable for me anymore.
I had to dig into the depths of my being
And harness all the strength I was made of
To make myself feel good again
To make life fun again.

I screamed at the sky for it to listen to me
And all I got in response were clouds
Wafting heavily
As though to serve as a reminder:
"Life will go on."

—You're Gone

It's easy to desire things:
A walk-in closet
A car with good suspension
Your skin on mine

The difficult part
Comes along with the heart
And the desires it keeps
Inside

—Detaching

I will always look for you among the crowd

I could be overseas

Or deep underneath

In a submarine

—I will Still Look for You

She wore flowers in her hair
And hated the confused stares
So sometimes she would pretend she was the only one alive

Just her

And her flowers

And her palms joined in prayer.

–Solitude

She dreamed of people
Before she met them
So when she finally did
She already knew who
And what
And when.

She dreamed of places
So when she got there
She would act surprised,
Sometimes even tricking herself.
"Was this in my mind's eye?"

You're a prophet, darling.
In your own little way.
Precognition illuminates
Like a candle flame.

   —Magician

You probably still love me, he joked.

I do.

I told him this.

He started typing, and then stopped again.

Did I scare you? I asked

It's okay

It's okay to be scared to love

That's all it is at first

And then the seconds pass

And you sink into the feeling

And you love

And you love

And you love.

—Love and Fear are Opposites

I loved them like they were my sisters.
So when we broke up, I wept like someone had died.
I even wrote them a long letter, which I never sent
Highlighting all of the things I thought they did wrong to me.
I gave evidence, here and here.
Can't you see, I'm the innocent one!
Can't you see, I loved you fiercely!
Can't you see, I did right by me!

It was useless.
They had painted a picture of me in their heads
With splashes of dark blue and grey
And at one point
The ink spilled
All over the page.

Friend breakups are the worst kinds of breakups.
Boys are one thing.
Friends are another.
Because with friends
You drive along the coast
With a polaroid camera and a bottle of Coke
And you promise each other you'll never go

And when our friend Alex died
And you sat in the closet and cried and cried
I felt my own distraught and then
I took on your pain as my own.

    —*Dead Friends*

✷

So many names in my phone
So many faces in my head
Who are you --
I don't know any of you.

  –Social Media

And whenever my head hangs down low,
I pick her up and say
"No, baby. We have struggled way too long
and way too hard
to be feeling this way."

−Trials

✶

A RISING
THING WITH
WINGS

If I could tell the whole world something right now,
I would tell them:
Don't fear.
The pain that you are feeling is only as real as you create it
to be.
God is within you and is powering your heartbeat.
Quiet, listen.
Do you hear that?
Pumping through your veins and allowing your lungs to fill
with air?
That's a very powerful force, if it can do that.
So chill.
This experience will end.
But it is just an experience.
It's not the real deal.

The truth happens when we remember we're in an experience.
When we remember that powerful force.
It's so easy!
So easy.

Sometimes we don't think it's easy, because we're
experiencing the experience.
But when we step back, we can see:
It is very easy.

–Good morning

Once we can learn to control the mind,
We're good.
The sun rises and sets each day,
Illuminating everything with its glamour.
Always on schedule.

So, things are running smoothly.
Someone is taking care of it all.
Our job is to control the mind.

In order to guide the entire machine
Of consciousness
Back to the heart.

–Illumination

You cannot experience gain
Without first experiencing loss
Getting very familiar with it
Drowning in the shocking vastness of it.

They celebrate the warrior as she comes home from war
Bruised a little, hair matted, and eyes shining with passion.
She saved the whole city.
She wants nothing for herself.
She only wants to give her heart.

—She wears a Purple Heart

My friends always ask me when I'll cut my hair
I tell them
When rivers across California run dry
And when all the grass turns green for the winter
And when there are no bugs in the air
That's when I'll cut my hair

When it becomes possible to turn back time
And the blades of past mistakes
Are no longer cutting away
When everything in my life is fair
That's when I'll cut my hair

And until then, the way it will be
Is blowing in the wind, wild and free
Golden waves to match the shimmering hills
And more turbulent than the tides of the sea

—*Reminders of Freedom*

What's your zodiac sign? she asks me.

I look into her light blue eyes, brimming with inquisitiveness,

so sweet and bright.

It makes me smile.

I open my mouth and it turns into a laugh.

I don't have one! I reply

What do you mean? She says. When's your birthday?

June, I reply.

So you're a Gemini!

I don't have a sign because I feel them all, I reply.

The dark night of November echoes my Scorpio soul.

The uncertainty of March moves my Pisces butterfly.

The hot days of August roar to my Leo bold.

I am all,

And I am none.

At once.

—The Twelve Houses

If we want to fear, we have the free will to do so.
If we want to love, that is also our choice.
The Universe reciprocates with our desires,
So if you ask,
You shall receive,
Either by conscious or unconscious requesting.

You have power.
We are taught our whole lives to
Listen to our elders,
Our teachers,
Our government.

We are taught to obey,
To curb our divine play,
To lessen our desire to create.

My child, there is nothing to mitigate.
The secrets of the universe flow through your veins.
Attraction is not just a law, it is a Universal truth.

Your inner voice is the loudest there is,
Cultivating all perception around you, both space and time.
And there is a Being constantly listening,
A Being Divine
 You are constantly Connected to, without reason or rhyme.

   –Someone Is Always Listening

In the Spiritual world,

Beings do not have bodies.

In that Indigo place, we don't move.

We transfer.

At the speed of light,

In the blink of an eye,

We know that we are unborn.

Here, things are messy.

Full of lessons.

We have forfeited that Divine place,

So now we must pay.

—The Human Experience

Sound is vibration
And vibration is creation
So anything you think
Is anything You say.
And anything you Say,
Becomes a Thing you create.
In this way,
We are a microscopic mimicry
Of God's divine play.

A picture is worth a thousand words,
That's why
Speech,
Which is first thought,
Has the potential to create worlds.

    —Infinitesimal

I do not fit in with others.

I look around and I ask questions

I like to invent,

I like to create.

I have never fit in with others.

Like a multicolored bird,

In a sea of white doves,

I stand alone,

Floating above.

—A Rainbow Thing With Wings

I need everyone to wake up.
I refuse to see suffering here,
It is madness, it is delusion.
Truth is waiting for you.
Separation is the greatest illusion.

In fact, there is no separation.
This is the only Truth.
That is why love is the strongest,
This universe was built on the backs of it,
And so were you.

Love is all that exists.
When we try to concoct
A fake reality,
Built on the greatest illusion,
We end up distraught.

In the illusion of separation,
Envy is its first quality.
"You and I are different," we say.
I want what she has.

We create illusion,
And then we partake in it.
This is the greatest misuse of human life.

Abandon illusion.
Why partake
It is fake.
Black and white.

—I Prefer a Life of Color

My heart bursts with desperation.
It aches with the surrender
And determination
To free as many souls
As God wills me to.

Anything that is not love is falsity
It is time to be diligent.
On where
Our minds, hearts, and actions lie.
On our priorities.
And on understanding that
We are directly tied
By the umbilical cord of everlasting time
To the infinite Divine.

—Love Personified

I need you to know that you and I
Unseparated by body and mind
Are the same by design

I need you to know
That without love we don't exist
And neither does the figment of time.

−Time to Break free from Material Conditionings

Abandon your identification with your perceived Self.

You are all that is Unperceived.

You are perfect because you can never be created nor destroyed.

You are existing in this expression

For the service of

And by the will of

All That Is.

    —Power

You are made of magic,

To break norms like the casting of spells.

To abandon all previous belief,

Any belief you dislike

And to adopt your own-

Free,

Expansive,

Crafted for only your life.

Sadness is also a conditioning.

When the natural state of the soul

Is

Bliss

We can see just how far

This world has strayed from that.

—We have Gone too far Off-course

Define your goals like stepping stones.

One at a time.

Pursue each with enthusiasm and patience.

Enthusiasm will result in applied

Devotion,

Character,

And compassion.

This formula will truly lead you to successful

Accomplishment.

—The Sweetest Recipe

It is important that one pays attention to how their movements are.

If one is swift and steadfast, then they must work to be calm and cool, so that there is balance. If one is slow and deliberate, then they must attempt to be more quick. This is the nature of perfect balance.

> *−The Most Difficult and Necessary Thing to Cultivate Here*

It is important to keep the mind fertile through creation. Creation leads to life, while consumption leads to eventual weariness, and then death of the Self. If you are alive here on this Earth, you have a mission.

−Reminder

＊

I want to make people feel things.

I want to scream as loud as I can to drown out the numbness that echoes between the bones of those who have given up on themselves.

We deserve to feel everything.

The human experience is like childbirth,

Messy and blissful.

−Alive

The only time that exists is right now.

Get up.

Put on fresh clothes.

Honor the body that you have been given by decorating it.

Protect it.

Make it smell nice and use it for the One who has created it.

Breathe in divinity.

Exhale oneness.

You and the trees both need each other,

But the one that has a voice is too afraid to admit it.

Make your bed, open the curtains in the bedroom of your mind, and go for a run.

This life is yours to conquer.

No one can tell you otherwise.

–Bedroom of Your Mind

*

You have provided me with all there is for me to know.
At this point I will use this knowledge to the best of my
ability in order to uplift others
Higher
And Higher
And Higher
On the ladder
Of ascension.
O Lord of the Universe, with flushed pink cheeks, lotus
petal eyes, peacock feather in your hair --

Allow me to serve you always.

My only desire is to use this book,
My fingers typing on this keyboard –
My breath quickening in my chest –-
My heart fluttering in love and excitement,

To serve others.

For you are in everything and everyone, pervading always.
When I serve another, I am serving You.
You reside in the depths of my heart,
Where it is more wet than the Ganges
From stored tears of love
Waiting to be released
In a flood of ecstasy.

     —A Girl With Devotion

✴

In the inward breath is where You fill me with life,

And in the outward breath is where You take it away.

You are the creator and the destroyer,

And in the middle,

Where the two breaths meet,

And converge into one,

Inner going into the outer

And outer going into the inner

I find you,

And I can see how

You are the maintainer.

—Krishna

＊

The water that spirals down my bathtub

Has been so mathematically formulated

That it has equal parts of 3, 6, 9,

And which mathematician

Is also the greatest magician?

It must be the one

who Himself is time.

The one who begins and then swallows all things,

Only He who can create has the power to also destroy

With leaves falling off trees,

Or the end of a life,

You Yourself are karma.

And we are experiencing You in all your wonderful ways.

−*Kālā*

You disperse yourself, like the rays of the sun.

And shine at night with again your own power,

As the moon.

You recycle Yourself

Into a spiral

Again and again.

You are the birth after death,

The summer after a long winter,

The male and female.

Only when others know You,

Will they be so careful in their actions and thought.

So careful

As to

Never

Take for granted

The You that is everywhere.

—*Yin and Yang*

✳

Each jewel
Came from the Earth
Same thing with the trees in my yard
And the selectivity in my heart.

Thank You for placing the Earth across your tusks
And for impregnating every form of life with your potency,
Down to the very last detail.

You have not missed a spot,
And after you created all the spots
You yourself came down to amplify your extension into
unlimited forms

To fill both the spots
And the spaces
Between them.

> —*You are in and in-between every atom*

In Kindergarten I used to talk about You

To anyone who would listen.

I remembered you like a very close memory.

When I was eight I started to properly meditating,

Crying childlike tears in missing You.

You are my best friend,

My ancient lover,

And my mother and father.

And even when I was in the womb,

I was next to You.

You keeping me close,

And me knowing it to be True.

Now I am a lot older,

And there is not a second that goes by

That I am not in agony while not remembering You.

—Remembering Krsna in the Womb

You complete me, and fill me up,

So you make it as if I need no other lover.

When I carry the Divine with me, I am not here in this body.

I am infused with Your radiant Holiness,

And my mind and heart form one single path.

Converged, You begin to flow out from me.

Through my tears.

Through my words.

Through my laughter.

I am a clear vessel, like a window,

Shining Your light.

–Bliss

Your ability to stay grounded is your gift.

Your ability to ground yourself before making any decisions is your gift.

Carefully scrutinizing and analyzing the situation,

Checking in with your higher self to tune into a space of peace

before executing any external reaction.

Your connection with the Universe is a gift.

Keep Him close and ask Him questions.

He will answer.

    —Telephone Intuition

Allow yourself to sink into your emotions

A diver does not go deep by staying on the surface

The true treasures worth discovering lie at the bottom of the sea.

Further and further down we go,

With each exhale removing another hold,

Into the abyss of what it means to truly Be.

Do not be afraid to feel.

It is in the feeling that we are discovering.

How else will we write great memoirs of our adventures,

With our scuba gear keeping us alive,

As with delve into the depths of the human mind?

Every turn, every twist, every heart-wrenching drop

Is but another opportunity

To sink and deeper and deeper

Into the land of discovery.

—If you're going through hell, keep going

Prayer

Is directed positive intention.

Its whispers form in the early hours of the morning and the deepest quiet of the night –

Asking. Imploring. Inquiring.

Once you put your order in, you step back.

Faith is letting go of your request.

And knowing that the system needs process it,

Convene with the kitchen,

Talk to the waiter,

And only then deliver your desire to you.

And only when

It can be catered.

–Chef's Special

Discipline does not operate based on inspiration.

Inspiration is fleeting,

And so it must be sparked whenever possible.

But discipline is its heavy opposite.

Dark, cold, and hard like metal,

Discipline makes up the barebones of all foundational structures,

Sturdy skeletons on the backs of which culture is built.

Religiosity and morality alike

Need discipline to survive,

And then get fueled by its counterpart –

Inspiration, to thrive.

–Twins

Power is the execution of knowledge.

Candle-lit nights spent pouring ink onto carbon paper,

We hammer it into our heads that we must be smart.

But wisdom is seldom found within the confines of our mental chatter,

And reveals itself to us once we exist in silent solitude.

The ego has nowhere to go when we shine a white hot spotlight on it,

And as it begs for its release, I smile triumphantly.

You are under my control now, I whisper.

The candle flame is blown out

By the gust of wind that is my relieved sigh.

There is no longer anything I am held captive by.

—Fire

✦

A FLYING
THING WITH
WINGS

I'm a clairvoyant,

An empath,

A public speaker,

A writer,

A daughter,

An intuitive,

A healer,

A lover,

And a giver of a joy.

I am also a receiver.

The two balance out.

And thus I become
Nothing.

　　　—Egoless

And in the middle of the night,

When all else is asleep

My mind makes the decision

To become very steadily awake

Light shines the brightest in the darkness,

As do the flashes of pure light that glimmer before my eyes

In confirmation that I am on the right path.

This beautiful energy carries me

Into deep nudges from the Beyond.

I am a vessel of communication and information,

As my heart flows across the paper in the form of ink.

I gather information from this realm and the next

Weaving the pieces together into a large quilt of constellations.

My pen moves faster and with more emotion

As my soul begin to dance, backward and forward

In a steady flow

Mirroring the movement of all the universes combined.

—Quilt of Constellations

The present moment is my strength.

I dig into the depths of my roots like a single rooted tree.

Into the energetic ancestry that makes me to be me.

I dig deeper until I feel the base of the tree underneath my feet,

And further still until my head touches the place where my feet would be.

I am in the place where light has had to take a different form to be able to reach.

Grounded, I am nurtured by the richness of her smell and the coolness of her breath.

I look around and I realize that I am within Her earthly breast.

—*Plant Medicine*

Good things happen in things of three.

Like you, yourself, and your divinity.

It is time to step back into your power,

Evening the score by listening to the compass of your heart.

It is your tour guide on this crazy ride.

With only your best interest in mind.

—Heart Compass

✶

Just as a baby bird cries for its mother,

Eyes closed, with the faith that all comfort will be provided,

The same way I am longing for You.

—Devotee

When I am 83

And my bones are not working properly

When my hair is barely there

And my teeth are no longer holding,

I will find joy in the moment –

Remembering in my soul the engraving:

That time is part of my body,

And consciousness is part of my everlasting mind.

I will rejoice in the knowing

That it is not what happened in my life – it is how I reacted

And I will live in peace

Knowing that my ego is a culmination of the people and
experiences I have surrounded myself with,

And that I have made the house in my mind a castle,

Always tending to its gardens,

Always watering the sunflowers that face

The radiant joy that is my spirit.

–A Promise to Myself

You love them because you understand them.

But love is borne from purity,

And nothing else.

So love them, dear, no one can stop you except yourself.

Love strongly, and do not get in your own way.

But that is your only duty to them.

How selfish it would be

If you decided to give that love to only one person

And not the rest of the world.

—Your love is a Precious Gift

✳

And when you get so tired of everything in this life

Remember that you are just here to learn the lessons

And relax

Because by being human, you are already on your spiritual

journey

There is a reason you came here,

And there is a reason you will go.

But until then, during the ride,

Remember to stay in the flow.

The more things we release,

The lighter we feel.

The lighter we feel,

The higher we climb.

The higher we climb,

The better we fly.

–Soaring

And at one point
My heart was so cold
I could have easily just
Put it in my cup.

—Sad Girl Juice

✴

Wish nothing but good
Unto the ones who wished you bad
The power of love
Cancels out sins
Of both you and them
For this life
And the next.

—Forgiveness

I cannot be angry anymore
I have exhausted every lasting possible piece of anger within
me
Wrung out and hung up to dry
And all that's left within the core of my being
Is a bucket of empathy
That stretches as far and as deep as the ocean.

   –Finally I am at Peace

Healing is not a battle.

It is only when we are resistant to healing

That we create a battle.

—Surrender to It

To move into a state of limitless expansion

Or limitless reward

We have to be willing to let go

Of all inhibitions tied to the ego

Sacrifices are made by those who are fortunate

And fortune always favors the bold.

—Much needed sacrifices

✦

You are only as healed as you believe yourself to be.

Whatever your belief is

Is your truth.

—Abracadabra

Keep moving forward.

That is your only instruction here on this planet.

Whatever you do,

Keep moving forward.

You don't need a manual,

You make the rules.

Welcome to the most advanced game you will ever play.

You're the main character.

—Simulation

＊

The language of thought
Is so subtle
That it does not need
To be made tangible
For every single being alive
To experience it.

—Blanket of consciousness

Every single living creature

Just wants to be comfortable
So relax, unfurl your brows.
Dance a little
Get that good feeling going in the space beneath your
bellybutton.
You have much to create here during your lifetime.

—Let go of your worries because they don't even exist

Right now I'm laying here on this beach

In the sand

Writing this book.

And one day, I'll look back and remember

All the little moments that I fell into.

Some of them will escape me,

But that's where I'll let them live

In the akashic subconscious

Of all that is.

—How mere thoughts become ideas that change the world

I have been through so much

In my very short lifetime

I had to pick up the pieces of both my brain and heart

Over and over again

So when I did it for the last time

I took a shattered piece and held it up to my eye

And whispered

Girl,

I'm going to give you all your desires.

—Fierce Protector of my own Dreams

She walked with long legs

And long hair

And long arms

And a long smile

That stretched from the East coast to the West

And which healed both itself and the rest.

She had high cheekbones

And bunny rabbit teeth

That hated being hidden

And loved being seen.

—I will be Here for Both Myself and You

I am not a reliant friend.

Do not rely on me.

I will teach you

How to rely on yourself.

—Fish for a lifetime

＊

Sadness is addictive.

Happiness is innate to our soul, but everything around us is

teaching us to be stuck.

And sad.

And in a state of addiction.

The biggest revolution you can engage in

Is fierce self-protection

Over your own heart, mind, and

Mood.

Protect your vibe at all costs.

—*Sweet rebellion*

My parents sacrificed themselves

So I could comfortably live a life

Of luxurious imagination.

  —Gratitude

✹

The world is too loud

How about we all calm down

There is a lot of goodness that comes in calm

The ocean on the surface is turbulent

But deep below

It is calm

Fostering life, fostering depth, fostering the natural cycles of things.

Push and pull, said the moon.

And the tide responded.

But deep below the surface,

All remains still.

Not even the moon can touch the protected land.

—This is where the magic happens

Even the heat of summer

Cannot drown out the chill in my bones

That sends shivers up my spine

When I think of the person I used to be.

—People Change Faster than Seasons Do

With each new person I fall in love with,

I remind myself

That the one who loves the most

Is always the one that needs it the most.

If all the clouds in the sky exhausted their rain,

What would happen to the trees?

The earth would turn brown and dry.

This is not the natural order of things.

I will not allow my heart to turn brittle.

—Self-love Will Always Come First

As I inhale deeply,

All the planets in the solar system pause their orbit.

As I exhale slowly,

They start spinning again, on their own.

As I hold my breath,

The moon and the sun freeze in their cycle,

Waiting for me

To begin once more.

—Planetary Influences

＊

Death to ego
Is the birth of love
My ego has died so many times,
That now my heart is floating in my body
Untethered and wild to beat
Any which way it chooses.

—Boundaries are a Protective Kind of Cage

✴

I woke up this morning

With the birds looking at me funny.

As if they understood the hopeful stirs of my mind.

Get back to work, they chirped loudly.

We rise with the sun, and

You are one of us.

  –Healing is a Never-ending Story

You are the main character

In the story

Of your life.

  —What Does Your Script Say?

All the crying in the world

Cannot bring back lost time

Do not even bother

Unless it is for the sake of cleansing

There is no need for tears.

The soul has everything it needs.

Rejoice in the composition of who you are

That pure energy is compassionate and humanitarian.

And so beautiful.

Do not be afraid to feel happy

While feeling it.

—Avoid Numbness at all Costs

With razor-sharp scissors

I cut many things away from me:

People,

My hair,

My sense of self.

I worked hard to get where I am.

I moved.

I changed.

I took off one old flesh suit and jumped into a new one.

I felt the deepest pain possible

And realized that others felt this too

And wanted nothing more

Than to use my newfound truths

To cut that away from the world, too.

   —*Compassion*

Let people say what they say about you.

That is their own sweet truth.

They have the ability to change it themselves.

But once it rolls off their being and into yours,

It can become your truth.

Sweet or not.

—Only Listen to Yourself and no one Else

If we all spent time

Judging one another

The amount of time wasted

Has enough energy

To power the illumination

Of the revealing moon.

—We are all Foolishly the Same

✸

When the universe wants you to sit down
And chill out
It will get you off your feet and on your behind
It will make you close your two eyes and open your third
The only one that can see inward
Into that which void of all illusion
And full of truth.

—Look inside for Happiness and Growth

✷

Love breeds creativity
Fear blocks it
Focus on that which feeds your soul.
Not on that which steals from it.

—White Light

We are infinite beings who have been given the opportunity to experience this human life. What a blessing everything is. Joy is our birthright. Pure, innate, childlike joy is what you really are.

Our physical reality is a projection of something we have already agreed to, and are constantly agreeing to, moment by moment.

This universe was created by means of sound - and sound is vibration. We don't have control over much, but we have control over the frequency at which our consciousness vibrates.

The highest vibration we can achieve is a state of pure, unconditional love All Things (aka, the Divine). Loving in this way is called prēma Bhakti. To live a life full of joy, in this way, is your birthright.

It's my dream that all human beings on this Earth live in a state of bliss and coexistence, recognizing their innate birthright to feel happy and free.

And overall, recognizing the innate truth of their soul.

   —*Sound Vibration*

✸

Author's Note:

Spiritual strength is something that can never be taken with us.
it is knowledge that embeds itself deep within the sweet
receiver, to remain with us throughout lifetimes. It is not
reliant on anything external or temporary to justify its
power. It stands alone, justifying itself.

There was a period of time in my life when I went through
some massive changes as a being. This transformational
period brought me to such a humbled state, that I found it
difficult to even order food at a restaurant. my ego went with
my sense of self, and all that was left was an open vessel for
information to enter into.

In our present society, this example is not always beneficial,
as it highlights a very extreme and temporary case of an
ego-death. In truth, the ego is meant for us to use as a tool
in order for the soul to spiral upward on the path of spiritual
progress. That's what we came here to do - in a human body
- to begin with.

We are powerful beyond measure, but it is not because
of any externalities that are present here in the material
world. Our power lies in our surrender - our surrender to
Source, recognizing our humble and meek position, and
never forgetting the beauty and the bliss of where we stand.

–This is What we are Made Of

Everything is our teacher if we are willing to learn. It's just a matter of seeing life objectively as a series of lessons to help our soul grow on the path of ascension. This life is a journey, and there's so much more before and after it. Once we realize that we idealize the importance of our experiences based on the emotion attached to it, we can pick and choose which experiences we want to keep close to our hearts.

–Discernment

The story we tell ourselves about who we are is who we become. We define our own limits and set our own standards for success. We don't know what we have the ability to love until we try new things and put ourselves in uncomfortable positions. The only reason for us being here is to grow, anyway. And the cool thing is, we help ourselves by helping others and vice versa. It's cyclical.

—*The Heart Center is the Control Room for all Positive Operations*

We attribute various meanings to our lives. If we act without meaning then we are doing ourselves a great energetic disservice. There is always a great operative reason for everything, including (and most importantly) our own existence. When we realize this, we will never be lost.

–Living a Meaningful Life

My opinion on the way we should approach controversial topics, especially ones that have to do with autonomy. What I've discovered over my years is that mindfulness and self-love are conjoined, and if we choose to, can promote our own protection. It's good to trust, but it's smart to do it with guidelines.

—Trusting with Boundaries

Sad can be beautiful too. It depends how we choose to look at it. We wouldn't know light if we didn't know darkness.

—*Stars Shine in the Darkness*

Controlling your thoughts and pruning them to make sure they are constructive and positive is something that I often struggle with, but is simultaneously the most precious and necessary thing that anyone can do for themselves. Controlling the way you see situations allows you to potentially change them from an energetic standpoint. Everything in life is a gift, even the hard stuff, which are lessons. These are the best gifts, the ones that help us learn.

—*Always Remember to Never Forget*

If someone doesn't understand you, don't waste your time in trying to explain yourself to them. They will take what they can and give you what they can. People are tricky. Relationships are tricky. It's best to know oneself so we remain stable and always come from a place of love and compassion. We're all just a work in progress. Myself too.

—*Stay Grounded and Approach People with Love and Tact*

✳

Every great piece of art is made with love directed in some form: emotion, rationale, thought - creative energy at the very barebones of it all. This creative energy that flows through us ties us back to source. Every living soul yearns for it, and we can search for it in the duality of everyday life, only to realize it exists back at the origin.

—We are Natural Creators

We are comprised of everything and everything is comprised of us. Let me know what you think about this, all of our thoughts come from the same mind anyway.

−Telepathy

We are the sun, the sea, and everything in between. All prayers to the Most High, who is always within us.

—Always trust

The way I got over heartbreak was realizing that I allowed my own heart to break.

Taking your power back is necessary, and keeping it is even more vital.

Anyone can break our heart. Any situation can hurt our emotional body.

We don't have to let it hurt more than it needs to.

We don't need to over-romanticize or hyper-ignore the pain.

It will always be a lesson,

and a lesson is always beautiful -

once it is learned.

—Heartmaking

The ways in which we allow ourselves to be free are crucial to maintain, day by day, for overall self-understanding.

The body ages, the material things wither away, and even intelligence is fleeting if it's not tied to the heart.

Break all chains of conditioning.

Surrender to the beauty that is your energy.

-—It is ever-present and Flowing Within You

The soul is Amal(अमल), or pure. If you're alive, you have a soul encased in a human body, as dictated by ancient Vedic scripture since time immemorial. To care for the soul means to live in a way such that the soul is able to shine through our individual self-expression. It means living from a space of truth, which is living from a space of love. Pure, unconditional, unrestricted love.

–World Beyond Matter

There is nothing to fear except fear itself, which is the greatest of all the disillusionments of mankind.

—Do not over-identify Yourself With Illusion

The highest caliber of human existence is loving service, which comes from the heart and which is of pure bliss.

This is how we can provide value to every single living being that crosses our path. This is how we can uplift the whole world.

−Highest Caliber

When we forgive ourselves and others, we allow ourselves freedom and we give the pain to God while we take the lessons from the situation.

—Lessons are Blessings

Ask yourself if the intention is pure.

Then ask yourself why you're not following your dreams.

After that, remove everything that gets in the way of your dreams. And if you're getting in the way of yourself, baby.

Step aside and

Let it rain.

—Rain on Them

＊

Humility and self-appreciation are not on opposite ends of the spectrum. Rather, humility is in itself the act of self-appreciation, because the deep love that we feel in our state of humility breeds this appreciation for the Self beyond understanding.

—An Ode to Humility

We all have a purpose here. As living beings in a human form of life, we have the ability to live out a legacy in the service of others. Service is the highest form of bliss and enjoyment, because it is internal bliss, which can never be taken away by anything external. The definition of a life path is that which serves the collective.

What do you think yours is?

−What is Inside is Waiting to be let Out

An Anecdote on Belief

We make everything that happens to us and around us in our head. We make it all up in our mind's eye. These experiences are projected by us. A man on the side of the street can either be a regular stranger or a sadhu based on the power of belief.

Belief is the strongest thing there is. If you believe your limbs are thick, long, and beautiful - then they will be. You also have the power to believe the contrary. This is a prime example of manipulating our vision of the object with our thought. And when the vision of the object is manipulated, the object itself is revealed to the human being as being manipulated, because we rely on our physical senses to navigate the world around us.

Farther behind the senses is the mind, which controls all things in our perception based on the power of thought.

Conscious thought is recorded, which is stored in the subconscious, and which in turn regulates the perception, creation, and integration, of all of our experiences.

The way the water swirls down the drain is the way my chakra energy centers swirl in my body, when I place my hands on them in an effort to quickly retune them.

The pattern in which water droplets bounce off of a subwoofer is a particular action which is governed by the exact same frequency that all things in nature tend to form patterns into.

Please do not forget that your life is a culmination of your beliefs.

An Anecdote on Vibration

Patterns repeat. they are geometrical and are all integrated and connected with one another, forming a grand composure of All That Is.

Additionally, the universe was created off of sound, which turns into vibration, which structures patterns, and whose patterns give off lasting results (this is what thermodynamics is about).

Physics is not a concept that is separate from quantum physics, and quantum physics really is just math at its core, and math is just numbers that formulate certain functions. Numbers are just information. And information is two things: light and sound. Light and heat are correlated, but sound is dependent on nothing – and correlated with everything.

Because sound creates consciousness, and consciousness creates rational thought within the universe, we are actually very cerebral beings – with deep roots to all sources of information. The Universe is actually all information, as well as the beginning and end of it. so, in this way, the Universe can be understood as: sound, light, heat, emotion, vibration, mathematical formulas, and combustion (see: thermodynamics).

So it's very easy to control the world around us when we understand ourselves in this way. just fragmented byproducts of Source and all of His creation, which is fractal.

A Birthday Letter to Myself

To the little girl inside me that just did her 22nd lap around the sun:

I'm relieved that you consistently choose love no matter what. I know you've been hurt by others so much in the past (who hasn't?) and now you don't need to worry about that anymore. It is a selfish thing to be hurt, instead of recognizing the pain in others and wanting to heal it. Seems, please stay grounded and remember that everything that you've been given has been given to you by God for you to give to others. Seems, never stop giving. This is your job. Never be afraid to give. You know that fear is something we're taught here, and that it doesn't rest initially within our spirit. Seems. the hardship brought you to your knees and forced you to reinvent yourself. I'm proud of you for the way you performed under the pressure.

You've changed: you've become transparent. Honest. Lighthearted. Funny. Intense. Real. Deeply feeling global compassion. Do not be afraid to show the world who you are, because you have been working on yourself for a very long time. There is nothing to hide. Seems, remember when you were told to stop "being a humanitarian" because "you can't save the world"? I'm so glad you didn't listen to them at that time. I'm so glad you took their words with grace, felt them, and then felt your own inner compass more strongly.

Seems, thank you for giving up things that no longer serve you, and giving up giving your energy away - especially mentally. I'm proud of you for repairing your relationship with your parents. I'm proud of you for gently loving old friends from afar. I'm so proud of you for starting your YouTube channel, because I know that was hard as hell. I'm proud of you for pouring your heart out onto your keyboard through the late nights by the candle flame and into the early mornings by the first shades of dawn. I'm proud of you for being your own support system when you didn't have one. I'm proud of you for re-parenting your inner child. I'm glad that you know what you want, and I'm glad that it's not just for you. Your heart beats for the collective, Seems. Protect it.

And don't you forget it.

Author Bio

Hi, my name is Seema and I'm the girl behind A Rainbow Thing with Wings. I am so glad you're here. Here are little light bits about me. I enjoy writing, calligraphy, video shooting and editing, singing, public speaking, dancing, and acting! I've done theater my whole life and would love to audition for a movie that I'm in charge of directing. I always (still) do funny skits at home to make my family laugh, but they would have to pay me to post the footage! I love to dance and I've only taken hip-hop and Bharatanatyam, but I would love to take more classes. love to journal and heal my mind through writing. I also love poetry (as if it wasn't clear enough) and I have notebooks filled with just my poetry! I'm also really into singing -- when I was 11 someone told me that my voice was "too soft" and since then I've sang every day to practice getting better. I definitely would love to be a professional someday, but I would need a coach. I also love the beach dearly and plan on living by the beach in my life. Ever since I was a child, it has undeniably calmed me and made me feel at home. I also love the moon, love sunny and warm days, and adore adventuring - even if it's just in the backyard. Making my friends laugh and laughing with them makes me super happy and is the ultimate stress reliever. I also love meditation and can get lost for hours in it! I have to set an alarm on my phone to gently lift me out of meditation. This is also how I trained my mind to focus on large tasks for long periods of time. I used to be fairly bad at focusing before I started meditating, or so I thought. I'm a huge believer in compassion and can feel things very strongly. This is why it's important for me to cleanse often with salt baths and stuff, but more on that later. I love candles, I love puppies, I love new clothes and early mornings and neon lights and fruit. And I love you, dear reader. Okay, bye for now.

FÍN
(अन्तः)

www.ingramcontent.com/pod-product-compliance
Lightning Source LLC
LaVergne TN
LVHW051401080426
835508LV00022B/2918